Understanding

Faith

*calling those things which be
not as though they were.*

Julian McClain

iUniverse LLC
Bloomington

UNDERSTANDING FAITH
calling those things which be not as though they were.

iUniverse books may be ordered through booksellers or by contacting:

iUniverse LLC
1663 Liberty Drive
Bloomington, IN 47403
www.iuniverse.com
1-800-Authors (1-800-288-4677)

ISBN: 978-1-4917-0174-4 (sc)
ISBN: 978-1-4917-0175-1 (e)

Printed in the United States of America

iUniverse rev. date: 01/11/2014

Foreword

I did not set out to write a book about faith. The reason I did so is because, one day while I was at work, the Lord said to me "Now that you have the splinter out of your eye, go help your brother." I had no idea of how I could do this, until one day my realtor and I a born again child of God, set out to buy a house. In sharing with him things the Lord had taught me about faith. He said to me, "You should write a book, so it would help others." I did not think much about it, but at work I began to see it and write an outline for it. I went home that weekend, wrote 10 pages and never looked back. The Lord has put three other books in my heart to write which I will. It is funny how our father God does, what he does. And since I set out to write this book, he has given me greater understanding than I ever had. I prayed the Ephesian prayers and I began to hear and understand through revelation, things of faith. I know that if you the reader will believe and put these things to work, the word of God will work for you.

In The Beginning
Part One the Definition of Faith

I had woken up at four o'clock as always to go to work praying in tongues, cleaning up, and drinking my coffee. I spoke to the Lord before going out the door "Lord come and go with me as I go to work today." Inside of me he spoke back, this was not as always, this time the lord spoke back to me telling me that what I was doing and saying was not faith as I had thought. As a teenager I had a dream that I was in a war, in which I was shot in the head, and at that time all of the dreams that I was having came true, so I felt that this one would too. Yes, I was scared, who wouldn't be? I went walking one day in an open field looking up. I said "God, I dreamed that I was in a war and got killed, a man can't get around his death. Come and go with me and I will face it like a man."

At that time I believed that there was a god. I just didn't know him. That enlightening morning, he said "Stop saying that, that's not faith." I said "It's not? Then I don't know what faith is." I asked him "What is faith?" His answer was not what I thought it should have been. Most believers, Christians, Churchgoers, and the religious people would not have said what he said. He said faith is calling those things that be not as though they were. Most Christians, believers, and religious people, would say that faith is Hebrews 11:1 "Now faith is the substance of things hoped for, the evidence of things not seen." I now know that I didn't know what faith was, or how to use my faith. I had read books on faith but I didn't understand. What the lord said puzzled me all that day. I now know when you are confused; you think that you understand, so when the lord straightens you out, you feel confused, because you never knew what the truth was, or that you were believing a lie. So I told the lord you would have to show that to me in your word that I might show and help others. He said go to Romans 4:17 and read it. "AS IT IS WRITTEN, I HAVE MADE THEE A FATHER OF MANY NATIONS BEFORE HIM WHOM HE (ABRAHAM) BELIEVED EVEN GOD WHO QUICKENTH THE DEAD AND CALL THOSE THINGS THAT BE NOT AS THOUGH THEY WERE".

This was the beginning of my understanding of faith. I know that most believers, Christians, Churchgoers, and even religious people would say that this is not right. So here is my argument. Most believers would not want to do that (argue) because they say that it is not godly, but Paul did it (argued.) Read Acts 17:2, King James uses the word reason and the reference takes you to Thess2: 2 they use the word contention. The amplified uses the word reason and argued in Romans. The only reason it is an argument is because most people , and even you were taught that faith is Hebrews 11:1. By someone that was taught that, by someone that was taught that, by someone that was taught that, by someone who did not get it from GOD.

So you and them thought that the person knew GOD better than you, or they were better educated than you, but that does not make what they say right. Some think that the pastor knows more than all of his listeners and that's not right either. All that does is tell you that the pastor is their GOD. They quote their pastor and not the Bible, or the word that GOD says to them or shows them in the

Bible. God is never wrong, nor the Bible. God the Holy Spirit shows us according to a situation, to which people do not study, they let their pastors do that part for them. That's why they say that faith is Hebrews 11:1.

Here is my argument. How come they don't say that faith is Romans 3:28? In Romans 3:28 it is saying that faith is a law, and faith is a law. How come we don't say that faith is Eph. 6:16? Where the bible says that faith is a shield, for our faith is a shield, or that faith is a Spiritual force, and it is a spiritual force, because of the same reason I said above. Someone told them that and they did not ask the lord for themselves. A great man said "Before a person can speak on a thing, he must first define that thing." Now let us give a definition to the word faith.

As the lord said to me that faith and the word of GOD are in levels and degrees as is the anointing. But we will not get into that. We shall define faith and its meaning. Faith is calling those things that be not as though they were. So let's put this meaning in Scriptures. Romans 1:17 the part that says "the just shall live by faith." We shall replace it with the meaning. The just shall live by calling those things that be not as though they were. Let us go to Hebrews 11:1.] It says "Now faith is the substance of things hoped for the evidence of things not seen" again let's replace the word faith with the meaning as the lord had said. Now calling those things that be not as though they were is the substance of things hoped for, and calling those things that be not as though they were is the evidence of things not seen. Let's take the word substance; substance is what something is made of, is it not? So our words make things, as our father GOD did and does. Our confession is the evidence of it being.

(Verse 2) Calling those things that be not as though they were, the elders obtained a good report.

(Verse 3) Through calling those things that be not as though they were, we understand that's how GOD the father framed the worlds, so that things which are seen were not made of things which do appear.

Verse 4, by calling those things that be not as though they were, Able offered unto GOD a more excellent sacrifice than Cain.

Verse 5, by calling those things that be not as though they were, Enoch was translated that he should not see death. Enoch was saying that he pleased GOD so that God the father would take him.

Verse 6, but without calling those things that be not as though they were, it is impossible to please GOD the father. Now you can go on and read the rest with that understanding.

What this books intended to do is teach the reader the understanding of faith. Teachers give homework, so read the rest of Heb.11 and use the meaning I have shared. The start of victory is to know what a thing is or have a definition of it and the start of it all is revelation so let us start there with revelation.

THE REVELATION OF REVELATION

Now let us understand what revelation is. Or shall I say, what bible revelation is. The definition for revelation in the bible is found in 1st Corinthians. In 1Corinthians 2:9 it should be understood that revelation is knowledge, there are two kinds of knowledge, worldly and spiritual. Spiritual knowledge is higher than worldly or man's wisdom. Revelation knowledge is where Adam falls from to worldly. Revelation knowledge is supernatural, supernatural stop the natural laws and put something else in its place.

For example the birth of Jesus the virgin birth, Natural birth comes from intercourse of a man and a woman, but Mary had not known a man; Therefore the revelation to her was that the Holy Spirit would come up on her and cause her to be pregnant and have a child which was a sign of God to man as what God had said in the book of Isaiah.

1 Corinthian 1:9-13 it reads "As it is written, Eye has not seen nor has ears heard neither has it entered man heart (talking about his spirit not the physical heart) of man the things that God has prepared for them that love him But God has revealed them to us by his spirit: for the spirit search all things yes the deep things of God.

Here we are told that revelation comes from God the Holy Spirit. We also know that Paul never met Jesus in the flesh, but by revelation that in a vision on the road to Damascus and all that Paul taught was revelation and the prayers for revelation for the church in the book of Ephesians (ehp, 1:15-22. 3:14-21& Colossians 1:9-14) These were the three prayers that the late brother Kenneth Hagen taught the faith bunch. I believe they all have prayed and use in their ministries, which I used and began to get greater revelation that I have not heard from other but see by the bible that it is revelation truth. We must have a clear truth of revelation that is given by the lord himself to understand why you need revelation, bible revelation.

In Matthew 16: 17-20) Jesus taught about revelation. The full teaching starts in the 13th

Verse but we want to look at this from the 17th verse where Jesus has made it clear that he is asking, who do they say that he the son of man is? Peter answers, "You are the son of God" that is when Jesus teaches, where revelation comes from and what it does to the person that receives it. What the revelation does to the person who receives it, and how they become a different person because of the revelation which we will see.

Matthew 16:17. In the 17 verse and Jesus answered and said unto him "Blessed are you Simon Bar-Jona for flesh and blood has not reveled this to you, but my Father which is in heaven." and I say also unto you that you are peter and upon this rock I will build my church and the gates of hell shall not prevail against it.

19 I will give unto you the keys unto the kingdom of heaven and whatsoever you shalt bind on earth shall be bound in heaven: and whatsoever you shall loosen on earth shall be loosen in heaven.

20. Then charged he his disciples that they should tell no man that he was Jesus the Christ.

Now let's open up this teaching on revelation, first it is as Paul said, that it comes from the Father and not from flesh and blood meaning man. But it can come from a man that is why he told them not to tell any man just yet.

In this teaching we see that he was talking to Simon bar-Jona, because he had the revelation that Jesus was the person that GOD had said would come and was now here, and most did not know it. Simon did know who he was,

Simon was changed by this truth to become a different person not Simon but Peter, and because he had this truth all of hell could not prevail or win against him , and in the new person he now had authority to change things for his self and others here on the earth, where the kingdom of heaven is and the sons of God live by faith.

When a person gets that Jesus is the son of God and that he died for their sins they are charged. Because that is a revelation, with that revelation most people seek to be born again. What is born again? To be born into the family of God, as a child but grow into a son and all hell cannot prevail against us, it is as the bible says, we are more than a conquer. More on revelation.

Revelation of Understanding

Jesus said in Mark 4:23, "HE THAT HAVE EARS LET HIM HEAR", in this verse our lord is not talking about if or ears work, but understanding. Proverbs 4:7 it says "Wisdom is the principal thing; therefore get wisdom and in all your getting get understanding." Defining bible understanding. Again we must define understanding Bible understanding is to know how a thing OPERATES the revelation of understanding and what it means for a believer to having it.

The first level of understanding is: <u>NO</u> understanding, not knowing how a thing operates, you can't operate it knowingly. To get success every time you use it.

The second level of understanding is: <u>BAD</u> understanding. With bad understanding you operate a thing badly. And have bad success at what you are doing, using your faith.

The third level is: <u>GOOD</u> understanding, you would be able to operate a thing well, for you understand principals that operate it.

The highest level of understanding is CLEAR understanding. Eph. 1:18 says the eyes of your understanding being enlightened, we know that the eye must see clearly, or 20/20, vision

In Mark 4, Jesus talks about the parable of the sower. The parable of the sower and the soil which start in verse 3 show us the levels of understanding.

Mark 4:

3. Hearken; behold there went out a sower to sow

4. And it came to pass, as he sowed some fell by the way side and the fowl of the air came and devoured it up

5. and some fell on stony ground, and where it had not much earth; and immediately it sprang up, because it has no depth of earth

6. but when the sun was up, it was scorched and because it had no root, it withered away.

7. and some fell among thorns, and the thorns grew up chocked it, and it yielded no fruit.

8. And other fell on good ground and did yield fruit that sprang up and increased; and brought forth some thirty, and some sixty, and some an hundred. So lets look at the parable and break it open from the understanding

The first one had no understanding, so that what he had was taken from him, because he did not know what he had, nor how he had gotten it. So it was taken from him. Again He did not know what he had, nor could he operate it. So what was it that he had? He had the word of God. Jesus said, "The sower sows the word." With the word comes faith or you can say it this way, when you hear the word you get faith. He did not understand that the word operated on the principal of a seed, and all seeds have a time set to bring it's fruit, because he had no understanding of what he had, it could be taken from him which it was.

The second person in the parable had a bad understanding. Let's look at what happened to him. he could not endure. He could not operate long, he knew he had the word of God and that the word had faith in it, but faith operates by love, love endures, love is patient. (1Cor 13:4) he had no love to make his faith work nor did he know the laws of love. Therefor he operated it badly.(his faith)

The third person had a good understanding. He knew he had the word of God, and the faith of God, and how to use the faith of God but he didn't know the purpose of God. he made his faith get him riches and the lusts of his heart. Those things choke the word. Those things choked his faith. his faith became unfruitful, and they shipwreck his life.

The fourth person had a clear understanding of the word of which he had received, that the word was full of faith, and what faith was, and what faith could do. It was for GODS glory. The person with a clear understanding knows what the word is, and how it works and that it has faith in it. They knew what their faith could do when used, They knew the purpose of it and it grew. Now ask yourself about your understanding, where are you? What is your definition of faith?

Understanding

We need to understand faith clearly. To understand faith clearly we must know the three parts of faith, and they are, Believing, Saying or Confession and third is your action on what you say you believe. we must have a definition, the definition sets the boundary of what you are talking about, Calling those things that be not as though they were. We should know what our understanding is. The understanding of having faith is, I HAVE THE ABILITY OF GOD TO CHANGE ANYTHING WITH JUST MY WORDS. This is what we are doing when we call things that be not as though they were, using our faith. Or GOD'S ability Before we go in to the three parts of faith lets see this in the Bible.

Mark 11:22; Jesus said "HAVE THE FAITH OF GOD." When we get our fathers word we have what the father has given to every person that is in the family a measure of his ability, to call those things that be not as though they were. As Abraham did when he had no children. (he called his self a father) Hebrews 12:2," Jesus is the author and finisher of our faith." (OUR ABILITY TO CHANGE ANYTHING WITH JUST OUR WORDS) or (CALL THOSE THINGS THAT BE NOT AS THOUGH THEY WERE) when any person is born again they receive a measure of faith of GOD or the lord Jesus. This is what some of the body of Christ don't know and that is why they live in defeat because they have no understanding of what they have. The ability of GOD, and because they

11

don't understand they think that they have to always ask GOD to do this or that. Why would GOD give you his faith if not to use it? for without faith it is impossible to please GOD. GOD loves us so much that he has not withheld anything from us, nothing.

Mark 11:22 Jesus said Have the faith of GOD. Can we have the faith of GOD? Yes Do we have the faith of god? Yes.

THREE PARTS OF FAITH

Mark 11:23 Jesus speaks, "FOR I SAY UNTO YOU THAT WHOSOEVER SHALL SAY UNTO THIS MOUNTAIN BE THOU REMOVED AND BE CAST INTO THE SEA AND SHALL NOT DOUBT IN HIS HEART BUT SHALL BELIEVE THAT THOSE THINGS WHICH HE SAITH SHALL COME TO PASS; HE SHALL HAVE WHATEVER HE SAITH."

In this verse, we find out what faith is made of. It is three things. **BELIEVING** and SAYING or CONFESSING and your ACTION, on what you believe. What is believing? Or believing according to the bible? The first part is believing. Let look at the revelation 0f believe

The revelation of believe has four parts they are **believe, unbelief, misbelief and no belief.**

Believing

Here again we have the argument of no understanding. Most people would say that believing is faith, that is not so. A dictionary would say the same but the dictionary isn't GOD or his word. What is believing? According to the bible? A preacher might say believing is faith. Again he got that from someone that got it from someone, that got it from someone that did not hear that from God using only his education. Please don't get me wrong an education is good, but GOD is best. The bible definition is what we are after.

In 2Chron.9: 5-6, the queen of Sheba spoke unbelief to King Solomon. "IT WAS A TRUE REPORT WHICH I HEARD IN MINE OWN LAND OF YOUR ACTS AND OF YOUR WISDOM: HOW BE IT I BELIEVED NOT THEIR WORDS, UNTIL I CAME AND MINE EYES HAD SEEN IT.

Believing is taking something to be the truth, even though you have not seen it or had an experience with it. Hebrews 11:6, part b of the verse, "He that cometh to God must believe that God is". We will put the meaning in this place of the word believe. He that comes to God must take it to be the truth that GOD is. Even though they have not seen him or had an experience with him. Just as we took the meaning and worked them in the places of the word faith so we will do the same here, used the meaning of believe. Do you take it to be true that God the father raised Jesus from the dead? Because you were not there to see it, that is why the word believe is used and not faith. The Bible says "All things are possible to him that believe (take something to be the truth.)." here in this verse we see how it is that a person believes. Believing is a choice the queen said "how is it that I believed not she choose not to, take it to be true. we must define the word truth to give a clear understanding. Truth the highest form of reality We must understand that the person that chooses, knowing that, lets look at unbelief

UNBEIEF to hear the word unbelief you would think that a person did not believe, and that is wrong here's why that is wrong. Belief is an act of a persons will, so it is not that they don't believe it is they refuse to believe and don't know that it's done by their will. In the gospel of john we see this from the mouth of Thomas the 20th chapter and verse 25 we'll start in the 24th verse

John 20:24-25

Now Thomas (called Didymus), one of the twelve was not with the disciple when Jesus came.

25. But said to them "Unless I see the nail marks in his hands and put my finger where the nail were and put my hand into his side, I will not believe. Here we see that belief is an act of the person's will, And in the book of numbers it was the unbelief of the children of Israel that keep them out of the promise land for they believe not what GOD had said about the land that he would give to them. The ten spies gave a bad report.

MISBELIEF

Misbelief is when a person thinks the bible says something that it does not say so therefor they think that they are believing the bible and are not, and they can be expecting something and get nothing because Jesus said if you believe what you say you will have what you say, but what you say is not truth form the bible do you get it? Let's look at misbelief in the bible in the gospel mark the 12th chapter from verse18-27

MARK 12:18-27

18. then came unto him the Sadducees, who say there is no resurrection : and they asked him saying,

19. Master, Moses wrote unto us. If a man's brother die and leave his wife behind him and leave no children that his brother should take his wife, and raise up seed unto his brother.

20. Now there were seven brothers and first took a wife and dying left no seed.

21. and the second took her, and died neither left he any no seed ;and the third the same.

22. and the seventh had her and left no seed; last of all the woman died also.

23. In the resurrection, therefore, when they shall rise, whose wife shall she be of them?

For the seven had her to wife.

24. and Jesus answering said unto them, do you not err, because you know not the scriptures, neither the power of GOD?

25. For when they shall rise from the dead they neither marry, nor are given in marriage, but are as the angels who are in heaven.

26. and as touching the dead that they rise have you no read in the book of Moses how in the bush, GOD spoke unto him saying I am the GOD of Abraham, and of Isaac, and the GOD of Jacob?

27. He is not the GOD of the dead, but the GOD of the living you therefore do greatly err so we See this group did not know the bible, so they were in misbelief.

No belief

Then there's no belief , all belief should be based on the bible, and what it says not on what a person think or a denomination teaches. No belief is a person does not know what the bible says about a subject. Nor can they believe correctly so that they get the victory of faith.

Saying

The second part of faith is saying or confession what one takes to be the truth. Here I must open the revelation of reality. By this I mean the difference in the levels of reality the definition of truth.

Truth

Truth is the highest form of reality. Even though you may not have seen it or experienced it If the truth is the highest level then there must be a lower levels. what is the lowest level? A LIE. WHAT IS A LIE?

Lie

The definition of a lie is, Something made up. The purpose of the lie is to fool, deceive, and trick. People lie to cover up things that they did or what they didn't do. The next level of reality is **fiction**

Fiction

The next level up is fiction. fiction is not a lie, because it is made up to be entertainment. It is not trying to fool, trick, or deceive. A lie tries to appear as truth when fiction does not. Then there is inference.

Infernce

Inference is what a person thinks about something, their personal opinion of something caused by a set of facts. That they take to be true; but truth is the highest form of reality. Truth does not change. Now we can come to a fact.

Fact

A fact is something that exists. What some people call facts can be put in with a lie and with inference. In a lot of books on faith the writer calls the word of God a fact they don't understand or have not the revelation of truth. I'm not putting them down because we have all been there. A fact can be a lying wonder as in Jonah when he was in the belly of the great fish.

What is a fact? A fact can be just information; it can be something that has happened. Jesus died, but he is not dead. The truth is he is alive. Jesus said the truth shall set you free. If the truth sets you free, from what is the truth setting you free from? A lie, a fact, and even inference. So what is it that keeps a person bound? It is what they believe, or what they take to be the highest form of truth, what they take to be real. It could be what they feel, or what they see or both. What it should be is the word of GOD.

Saying or confessing the word is the second law of faith , which is a very little known law. faith has a set of laws (romans 3:27) which I shall teach about later. the second part of faith, which is to say or confess as the truth. Christianity is called the Great Confession. Let's look at the book of Romans. Romans 10:9 say, "If you will confess with your mouth that you take it to be true that God the father has raised Jesus from the dead, and believe in your heart you shall be saved." That word saved is the word salvation which gives the believer any and everything that they the believer has a need of, which could be healing, recreation of a part of the body, or even bringing back to life. But you must believe or take it to be the truth. We must go and see what the word of God says, about confession.

Let look at the raising of Lazarus from the dead. In chapter 11 of the Gospel of John

In the Gospel of John when we look at the confession of Martha where she believed that Jesus could have stopped Lazarus from dying of which he could have but didn't because it was not the will of the Father, so that they the believer could see the power of GOD, That there was no situation that the power of GOD could not change. When we look into scriptures, we see that Martha confessed that she believed (the first part of faith) he would be raised (her confession) but in the resurrection starting in verse 20

The Gospel of John, 11:20-26

20. Martha, as soon as she heard that Jesus was coming, went and met him; but Mary sat in the house.

21. then said Martha to Jesus LORD, if you had been here, my brother would not had died.

22. but I know that whatever you will ask GOD, GOD will give it to you.

23. Jesus said to her your brother shall rise again.

24. Martha said unto him. "I know that he shall rise again in the resurrection at the last day.

25. Jesus said unto her I am the resurrection, and the life ;he that believes in me; though he were dead , yet shall he live.

26. and whosoever lives and believes in me shall never die. Do you Believe this?

27. she said unto him yes, Lord; I believe that you are the Christ, the Son of GOD, who should come into the world.

As we go and examine the verses we see many things but the main thing is what Martha believed and what she confessed verse 21 Martha faults Jesus with her brother's death, by not being there.

Verse 22, Martha states her belief in Jesus and GOD. That GOD would give to Jesus whatever he asked. Verse 23. Jesus tell her that he shall raise again. (because she is believing) verse 24. Martha tell Jesus she knows that but it will happen at the last day at the resurrection, verse25, then Jesus tell Martha that he is that resurrection, and explains the resurrection life, then Jesus ask Martha if she believes? Verse 27 Martha confess that she does believe what he has said, that her brother would raise again.

Then over in verse 39 they are at the grave of Lazarus, and Martha tells Jesus that Lazarus has been in the grave four days and by this time his body stinks, but verse40

40. Jesus said unto her , said I not unto you that, if you would believe you would see the glory of GOD. Also in this teaching is the ninth law of faith look not at that which is seen but at that which is not seen, which is to hold on to your confession.

Now let's look at another story that teaches about two of the parts of faith **believing** and **confessing.**

In the Gospel of Mark we have another story of faith where Jesus tell us to only believe in this story believe has to be held on to as in all faith fights, as it was in the last one and as it is in all faith fights. We look at the 22 verse in the fifth chapter of the Gospel of Mark

The Gospel of Mark 5:21-23

22. There came one of the rules of the synagogue Jai' rus by name and when jai'rus saw Him.

23. and he besought Jesus greatly saying my littler daughter lieth at the point of death. I pray you come and lay your hands on her that she may be healed; and she shall live.

24. And Jesus went with him.

In this story we see that it's one of the leaders of the synagogue and most of the synagogue was against Jesus, but Jai'rus needed his help, because he like the other leader had heard of Jesus healings. Jai'rus' s daughter needed healing, Jai'rus had come and begged for his help. Jai'rus believed in Jesus (part one of faith) he had two confession, 1. that Jesus would lay his hands on his daughter, 2. that she would live for she was at the point of death. The third part of faith is a persons action Jai'rus believed that Jesus could help so he went to him. Jai'rus had probable consultant a doctor who told him that he could do noting to help her, that is why Jai'rus went to Jesus.

The Lord was stopped by a woman that needed help and she told him her story of how she was healed. Her belief and confession and action for she had heard how Jesus had healed others and that she had gone to many physician and spent all of her money and was no better but got worse.

She believed that she could get healed her confession was if she would touch his clothes she would be healed. So she went to act on what she believed , she did what she had confessed and she was healed. But as she told Jesus her story there came someone from the home of Jai'rus and brought bad news that Jai'rus' daughter had died, and that he need not trouble the master.

MARK 5:35 While he (Jesus) yet spake, there came from the ruler of the synagogue's house certain which said your daughter is dead: why trouble you the master any further?

36. As soon as Jesus heard the word that was spoken, he said unto the ruler of the synagogue, be not afraid, only believe.

What was it the Jai'rus was to only believe? It was what he had confessed that Jesus would come and lay his hands on his daughter and that she would live even now when someone has come and said that she has died, the end of the story was as Jai'rus had believed his daughter would live and not die.

Now in Mark 11:23be healed and not die as the doctor had said. Jesus tell us the parts of faith and how faith works. It works by what you say, and continual to say till you see what you say

MARK 11:23.

Mark 11:23, Jesus said "THAT YOU SHALL HAVE WHAT YOU SAY," not what God says, not what Satan says but what you say. (**this is part of the Faith law teaching**) and what he is saying is an guarantee. If you can see this in the word Jesus guaranteed it, for he said, "You shall have it." Let's look at 2Cor. 4:13 with the meaning of those words so that we may get a clear understanding, the verse says,

"WE HAVING THE SAME SPIRIT OF FAITH AS IT IS WRITTEN I BELIEVE THEREFORE I HAVE SPOKEN. WE ALSO BELIEVE AND THEREFORE WE SPEAK." now let's put the word change in. "WE HAVING THE SAME SPIRIT OF CALLING THOSE THINGS THAT BE NOT AS THOUGH THEY WERE, ACCORDING AS IT IS WRITTEN. I TAKE IT TO BE THE TRUTH, AND THEREFORE I CONFESS IT TO BE REAL TO ME, WE ALSO HAVE TAKEN IT TO BE THE TRUTH, WE CONFESS IT AS THE HIGHEST FORM OF REALITY."

John 17:17. Jesus is talking to the father in prayer, he says, "Sanctify them through your truth; your word is truth." (The highest form of reality shall set you free.) Now we know that faith has three parts and what they are so we can now use our faith. I am ready to prove this by the word. Let's go to the Father of faith, and study what the lord has shown me. We shall see the believing and not speaking is not faith. This will prove that believing is not faith, as some would tell you why some use the word faith for the word believe. This will tell you that they don't understand, and if you are at that level where there is no understanding, your victory can be taken from you by the kingdom of darkness, and you are a victim.

In Genesis, when the lord started speaking to Abram, he was 75 years old; the lord spoke promises to him of the land in which the lord had appeared to Abram.

Abraham with No Understanding

Abram was full of fear. If you are full of fear, you cannot operate your faith. If you are in faith, you willnot fear. That's why he lied to the king of Egypt, not knowing really who GOD was, what God Would do for him for the lord had not made his self known in what he could do. The lord said that he; God would bless them that bless Abram, and he would curse them that curse Abram. If you will read the entire story, you will see that Abram was disobeying the lord. You cannot be disobedient and operate your faith, for the blessing is because you obey.

The lord had told him to get away from his people and his kinsman. After that Lot separated from Abram, the lord told him more of the blessing in chapter thirteen. In chapter fifteen, we see that Abram tells the lord that he is childless knowing the lord had told him he would give him seed after his self. Now notice that in verse 6 it says that Abram believed, what did he take to be the truth? (That he would have children) Here you see that believing without confessing what Abram believed is not faith. Some will say that believing is faith, but they were without understanding.

In chapter 17, God cuts the covenant with Abram. If you don't know the covenant and its understanding, there is an exchange where God changes Abrams' name to Abraham. The name means, "Father of Many Nations." Abraham begins to call those things that be not as though they were,

Abraham spoke the first part of the language of faith , which is **I AM**. Abraham now was saying that he was a father, he was calling thing that were not as though they were. **(Romans 4:17)**

At seventeen I did not know these things, all I knew was that I had dreamed that I was shot in the head in a war. I thought that meant I would be killed, but I didn't tell anyone. At that time I was a 4F; not fit to be in the army. I had been placed on probation for strong-armed robbery, but I believed that I would go to a war. I had gotten a job and was staying out of trouble, eventually my 4F was done away with, (of which I believed and was saying) I would joined the army. I did basic and A.I.T. training, and I was off to Vietnam. I had already been using my faith without knowing it; calling those things that be not as though they were, for I had been saying that the army would change my status to a 1A so I could go into the service. Not understanding faith and how to use it does not mean you can't operate it, because I did it unknowingly. I thought It was God causing me to say the things that I did. I arrived in Vietnam Dec Friday the thirteenth, in 1968, which most people think is a day full of bad luck, but there is no such thing as luck. The amplified bible proverbs 16:33 part b says "Even the things that seem accidental are really ordered by God."

As people tried to put fear in me, I wouldn't call those things that be not as though they were, negative speaking. I said we would land and I would make it to the unit that I was assigned to. I believed that it was God causing me to say the things that I had said; getting me to my unit then finding out that I would be sent out to the field where most of the fighting took place. I thought I was ready to die, and I was, until I had a vision, or what to call it that I had, All I knew was that I saw two women lying over a casket crying because of what I took to be my death. That hurt them and I spoke to God telling him that "I refuse to die here in this God forsaken place and I would kill any and everything that would try to kill me, on two, four, six, or eight feet." I said that I would lay down my life anywhere that he would say but not there, and those words ruled my life until I gave the protection of my life over to the lord. My confession now is, "If God can't protect me, I can't be protected."

Abraham calls himself—father of many nations for that's what his name meant and he had no children. This was his calling those things that be not as though they were. Abraham shared this with his wife Sarah before he and God cut the covenant. At the time there was no bible, but God told Abram to look at the stars and at the sand, that this would help his faith. That is why Paul wrote "Look not at the things, which are seen, but at that which is not seen." Our father was teaching Abram to understand faith. Abram was like most of us; we share our faith or what God has said to us with unbelievers. We as believers should not do this why?

When we share with the unbelievers what the lord has said to us, they may not believe in it or in you for that thing. So they speak their unbelief and it causes a war in the spirit realm, where the kingdom of darkness fights the kingdom of heaven. This helps to bring the answer in to this realm. How many people do you think thought that Abram was off his rocker? A 75 year old man and a 65 year old woman, having a baby. Paul said faith comes by hearing the word and hearing the word of God. That's why Sarai told Abram that it would be through someone else, expressing her unbelief. No! Abram heard right, he laughed when he heard it. If you will read the whole story and study it, you would see it. The word study means to investigate and seek out the truth. It is after Abram became Abraham and

Sarai became Sarah, that they were calling those things that be not as though they were. And when Sarah heard it she received faith and the ability to do as God had said. Sarah had began calling herself a young princess, which caused her body to change. She would have a child one-year later. Faith comes by hearing and hearing the word of God. She heard GOD say she would have a child.

Is anything too hard for our GOD? So now Abraham understands how to use his faith So lets see it! Isaac is born in the 21st chapter. Thirteen years later in the 22nd chapter God tells Abraham to take his only son and offer him as a burnt offering. In verse 5, Abraham calls those things that be not as though they were. Abraham says to the young men that are with him, I and the lad will go and worship and come again. What if the young men would say "Wait Abraham, how shall you come again with the boy if he is the burnt offering?" Abraham could answer, because faith is calling those things that be not as though they were.

Now this is about faith, so notice this to help you with your giving to God. Giving is worshipping him. Abraham said that we shall go and worship. I just felt I had to point that out to people who would look in the bible. Verse 7, this is where Isaac learned to use his faith. He said, "Look the fire and the wood, but where is the burnt offering?" Again Abraham calls those things that be not as though they were, for he says "God will provide himself a lamb for a burnt offering." Also notice that Abraham did not tell Sarah or any of the young men what the lord had told him to do. For Abraham built the altar, laid the wood on the altar, and bound Isaac. Abraham raised his hand to kill his son and the angel of the lord called to him. You know the rest of the story of faith. After Sarah's' death, Abraham continued to call himself the father of many nations taking another wife and having more children, chapter 25, read it.

I Refuse to Die

Those were the words that I had spoken to God because of the vision I had. Those words had to stand the test if they were true words of faith, or words of hope. Maybe words of hurt caused by what I had seen. I believed they were of faith caused by God. I had three experiences with death that I believe proved they were faith filled words. The first one came on a day that there was a firefight down by the bridge just outside of a little town by the name of Trang Bang. I was assigned to the 25th infantry division, the third of the thirteenth field artillery. The fire support base was Steward Three, and the fire support base set on a graveyard outside of Trang Bang. As shots rang out they came faster every second. There were two different shots, one was a pop and the second was a cracking sound. The pop was the M16 and the cracking was the AK57. As the shots were fired, I became eager to see more, for some down at the little bridge were friends

So foolishly I stood up on the eight inch Howitzer to see down at the bridge, but I could not see where the shots were coming from. Then for some reason I just got down and walked away. I don't know why, but I now believe that it was the providence of God. As I was walking away something touched me or hit me in my back. As I turned around to look, I saw someone else standing where I had stood, and that young man from Indiana was shot through his left eye the bullet coming out of the back of his head.

We caught him as he fell and he died on the way back to the base camp.

The second one came one night as I was doing phone watch. Phone watch is one person staying on the gun pad to listen for a call up. The infantry calls for the artillery to fire on a location where they think or know the enemy is. I was laying down sleeping on a cot having a dream and again, don't know why, but I got up and walked about ten feet away. When I realized that I had moved not knowing why, coming to myself I turn to see a Mortar hit the cot blowing it up, and not blowing up the gun powder that was three feet from it. Yelling in coming I started to run to get the other men out of the bunker. Again something stopped me, either the hand of God or the providence of God. Which one I don't know, I just thank God that it did. I would have been at the door of the bunker and would have been blown up, but again death could not take me for I had said I refuse to die here.

The Bible says that life and death are in the power of the tongue,(law 1 of the faith laws) and they that love it eat thereof. Proverbs 18:21 and Proverbs 6:2 say that you are trapped by the words of your mouth. The lord said in Mathew 12:37, "By your words shall you be justified and acquitted and by your words you will be condemned and sentenced." I was calling those things that be not as though they were.

The Blessing of God
(having what you said)

CALLING THOSE THINGS THAT BE NOT AS THOUGH THEY WERE is the faith of God. The lord said he would bless them that bless Abram, and he would curse those who curse Abram. We have seen that Abraham called his-self the father of many nations, and he is. Look at the blessing when Isaac gives it to Jacob, Isaac calls things that be not as though they were. We shall look at it in the bible. Genesis 27: 28, Isaac begins to call those things that be not as though they were.

GENESIS 27:28

"God gives you the dew of heaven, the fatness of the earth, and plenty of corn and wine." In verse 29, "Let people serve you and nations bow down to you, be lord over your brother, let your mother's son's bow down to you. Cursed be everyone that curses you, and blessed is everyone that blesses you."

We will study and compare the blessings. Look at the blessing that Isaac gave Esau in verse 38. Esau asks the question does Isaac have but one blessing? Then Isaac blesses Esau.

GENESIS 27: 38-40

"Behold your dwelling shall be the fatness of the earth and of the dew of heaven from above, by your sword shall you live and shall serve your brother and it shall come to pass when you shall have dominion that you shall break the yoke from off your neck." If you read the whole chapter you will see that Isaac gave Jacob the better blessing because he called him lord over Esau.

What things have you called your children? Call them good things, call them great things. If you read the book of Genesis you will see that what Isaac said came to pass. Jacob did not call his self-the new name that he had gotten until he was ready to die. That is when he really called those things that be not as they were.

In the 28th chapter genesis and verse 4 Isaac gives Jacob the blessing of Abraham. Jacob goes away and the lord makes himself known to him in a dream. The lord commits himself to Jacob to be with him. When Jacob awakes he commits himself to the lord and he vows to pay the tithe. Laban was the first to get the blessing and curse from Jacob. Laban changed his word to Jacob for Rachael and giving him Leah, Laban did the same thing when it came to the cattle and sheep, but we know the story. Laban knew that from the time Jacob came to his house that the lord had blessed him. So we see that who blesses Jacob became blessed and we see that when Laban cursed Jacob he then became cursed. Laban says this in verse 27 chapter 30.

In the 31st chapter of genesis and verse 2 Laban no longer looks at Jacob as being good for him because Jacob has increased and he, Laban has decreased not knowing that the blessing of Abraham is in operation, spoken by God,

Abraham, and Isaac. This is faith calling those things to be. Here is a thing that Jacob called to being in chapter 30 verse 33. Jacob says that his righteousness answers for him. His righteousness will be his pay,(right standing with god) Over in chapter 31 we find out that the lord had told Jacob how to do what he did. It was given to him by the lord spoken to him in a dream. When Jacob leaves, Laban comes to stop him and take all that the Lord had given him, but the lord comes to Laban in a dream just as he did for Abraham. He tells Laban that he shall take heed that he not speak good or evil to Jacob. Laban wanted to speak and take all that Jacob had for he called it all his. He was afraid of the God of Abraham and the God of Isaac. The Lord had made himself known to Laban. Jacob knew Laban would take that which was his by force, which Jacob tells him in verse 31 of chapter 30. In verse 32 Jacob speaks a curse unknowingly and Moses tells us this, that Jacob did not know that Rachael had stolen it. This is why I believe that she died early in her life. Then came the changing of Jacobs's name, which he did not do.

In chapter 32of genesis and verse1, the bible tells us that Jacob saw the lord coming with some angels. The word that the bible uses is the host of God and we know who the host of God is, Jesus. Also in the 32nd chapter Jacob wrestled with a man until daybreak. This man had to have had super natural strength for he touched the inside of Jacobs's thigh and it came out of joint. Still Jacob wrestled against him until the man asked to be let go. But before Jacob let him go the angel had to bless Jacob, which he did with the name Israel. As a prince you have power with God. The king James margin of the Scofield Bible says "he who strives with God." Here we must understand that a blessing can only come from one that is greater; the blessing comes down. So this man blesses Jacob and he lets him go but never uses the blessing, that was the name given to him. Chapter 35 verse 9, God appears to him saying that his name Jacob is no more but is to be Israel.

If you will look at the bible you will see that Jacob did not call himself Israel but two times that I could find, until his death. The Bible goes back and fourth from Israel back to Jacob, to me, that is in and out of faith. Then Joseph came along with a word from God, which he called those things that were not, which we know, came to be. Even after Joseph had been dead about four hundred years, we see that the blessing of God is calling those things that be not as they were, and is a form of prophecy. Jesus called those things that were not as though they were. In raising the dead, Jesus never said they were dead he called them sleeping. In the first account, is the daughter of Jairus, the ruler of the synagogue. Jairus called those things that were not as though they were in the amplified.

Jairus said, "my daughter has just died, but come lay your hands on her and she will come to life." Before they can get to Jairus' problem the woman with the flow of blood had called those things that be not as they were saying to herself constantly, "but if I only could touch his garment I shall be restored to health." In the King James Version it says Jesus said your calling those things that be not as though they were has made you whole. You must understand that you also must act on what you say. Now onto Jairus, they came to the house and the people said that Jesus was too late for the girl was dead. Jesus called her sleeping, why did he say that she was sleeping? Jesus called the dead sleeping to take the faith fight out of his mind. The faith fight is in the mind. (faith fight is to fight the sences) When we try to believe the word, the mind throws it out because the mind can only believe what it sees or feels and the other senses That is why your mind has to be renewed. You have to remember to rise and meditate, thinking on and investigating the word your believing. For if the mind thinks the person is sleeping it does not fight impossibility. Jesus put out the unbelievers because their unbelief could stop his, the mother, and the father's faith and ability to change things with just their words as God does. By speaking that she shall live, we see the girl did live.

In all cases the lord said they were sleep as with Lazarus in John 11:11. Lazarus is resting and sleeping but I am going to awaken him out of sleep. Then the Bible tells you that the disciples thought he meant a refreshing sleep not death. So he told them plainly that Lazarus was dead, calling those things that be not as though they were he gives life into things by calling them alive. With the fig tree Jesus said "no man eat fruit of you here after forever." Peter and the rest of the disciples took notice the next day that the tree was dead.

In the book of Judges, Gideon is called a mighty man of Valor. This is GOD calling those things that be not as though were. The story reads on that Gideon became the man that the lord called him, and on and on I could go with calling those things that be not as though they were. Jesus called those things that be not as though they were when he said "destroy this temple and I shall raise it up in three days." Here we must get in to how things work which is to go into understanding to understand what affect our faith

The Spirit of Religion

The reason that most believers don't understand is because of the spirit of religion. Many preachers talk about religion but most can't tell you of them or him. Who is the spirit of religion?

The spirit of religion is the third person in the UNHOLY GODHEAD. We the body of the lord have to understand Satan is imitating God the father. Which is the Holy GOD Head. Satan said I will be like the most high.(Isaiah 14:14) Let's look at the GODHEAD. The GODHEAD in the old testament was made up of three persons Jehovah God the Father, God the word which the lord became man, and the Holy Spirit. But after Jesus was raised from the dead, the GODHEAD became GOD THE FATHER, GOD THE SON, AND THE HOLYSPIRIT.

Then there's the unholy God Head, Satan the father of lies, the Anti-Christ, who shall be a man in whom Satan shall enter in to proclaim that he is God. and the spirits of religion. who is over denominations and it is different with each one.

All denominations claim to believe the bible from Genesis to Revelation, but each teach different things about different subjects such as baptism, being filled with the Holy Spirit, (which is the fullness of the Spirit) the rapture, and on and on. This is caused by the spirit of religion to divide and conquer and most of all keep people out of the body of Christ and from being part of the kingdom of heaven, and most of all out of prayer.

What is there you or I can tell God the Father that he doesn't already know? Nothing! God knows everything so why tell him anything? We should ask him things as David did. Most of the body of Christ does not know how to pray the Lords prayer; they just recite it, and think they've prayed. So why do we do it? Because someone that was told by someone, that was told that by someone, that did not get it from the Lord, who got it from the spirit of religion When we go and tell our problems to the father it makes us feel good, but the problem is still there, therefore we must hear from God. I work with a person that says that they are a Christian, but they says that God does not speak to man anymore, when she should have said that God doesn't speak to her. Now that thinking is against the word because God does not change, he talked to man but now he doesn't, well that's change. So either she's wrong or the bible is, I believe it's her. Where did she get that? The church that she attends where she says she is still backsliding.

The Bible teaches what the general will of god is for all. It is when we spend time with the Holy Spirit, he will tell us the thing that God the father wants for us is different from all the other persons in the family of God.

1th CORINTHIANS 2:9-10 the revelation from God

1Corinthians 2: 9-10 reads eyes have not seen nor ears heard, neither have it entered into the heart of man the things which God has prepared for them that love him. Jeremiah 29:11 says I know the thoughts and plans that I have for you. The Lord says the thoughts and plans for welfare and peace and not for evil, to give you hope in your final outcome. There are many more scriptures that I can bring up that say the same thing. This is how the spirit of religion operates, through ignorance, doubt, and unbelief. People not talking to their father God for themselves, thinking that the preacher is doing it when some of them are not even called to preach or teach the word. The word said that many false prophets are gone out. Some churches take people in telling them to read their bibles and pray. These are babies, that's like bringing home a new born putting them in a baby bed and saying to them your milk is in the refrigerator and your diapers are over there.

Let's just look at some of the things that the spirit of religion has done, and is doing in the church now. One of the things attacking the church is the abomination of homosexuality. Being homosexual or gay is wrong and it is clear in the bible. (LEVITICUS 20:13.) The spirit of religion has people saying that it is wrong because the lord had to destroy Sodom and Gomorrah because of the homosexuality that was going on there. To say homosexuality is wrong we must prove it and define it. Homosexuality is two men or two women having intercourse. The purpose of intercourse is to reproduce life, which is only a part of marriage to reproduce. You need a seed, which is only found in man, the egg or incubator, which is only found in women. Therefore you need a man and a woman to reproduce human life, anything else is wrong. But let me be understood no one is to live by what I believe but me , and if a person wants to do that or live that way they have the right to, for GOD give them free choice

Here are three reasons that our father and God would not kill or destroy man. First, God the father loves them and us, but they that were in the two cities of Sodom and

Gomorrah. Two, he knew that they were dead in their spirits, Three, their nature in them was to sin, and if God did that to them then he would be unjust. But God is love and that's his motive in all things at all times.

Let's see what the Bible says about Sodom and Gomorrah in Genesis 18:17. He asks should I hide from Abraham his friend the thing which he has to do. The lord blesses Abraham with the words that command his children and his house to keep the way of the lord that the blessing of the lord would come on Abraham, which he had spoken of him. He calls Abraham to a higher level of faith and anointing. The second level of faith is the priest, also the level of intercession. We are studying the spirit of religion and how it works in the life of believers with lies to stop the use of their faith.

The lord says that the great cry of Sodom and Gomorrah has come up to him with their sin is grievous. The lord says I will go down to see for his self that which is to come to him is true that he may know. Here GOD is seen as what he is LOVE

1John 4:16, God is LOVE. Love is the father's reason for doing all that he does.

1Cor 13:4-8. THE LAWS OF LOVE

Love is patient and kind, love is never envious nor boils over with jealousy, love is not boastful or vainglorious, and it does not display itself haughtily. Love is not conceited. Love is not rude and does not act unbecoming. Love does not insist on its own way, and love is not self-seeking. It is not touchy, fretful, or resentful; love takes no account of the evil done to it. Love pays no attention to the wrong done to it, it does not rejoice at in justice but rejoices when right and truth prevail. Love bears up under anything and everything that comes; it is always ready to believe the best of every person. Loves hopes are fadeless under all circumstances and endure everything without weakening. Love never fails.

Now those are the laws and the principals of love. Does God know everything? Yes! Did he know that what he heard was true? Yes! If God knew this why did he go to see, because of love. Love thinks the best about a person all the time. He was not thinking about the evil that was done against him as lord of the earth, and God was kind, because he got an intercessor that would turn away judgment that was to be done to them. Is that kindness? Yes! Intercessors are able with their faith and prayers to go to the father and change his mind as the judge of all the earth. remember faith works by love

Abraham did not take GOD far enough. He stopped at ten righteous when he could have gone to one, which was Lot. Because the sin of one man(ADAM) made all sinners and the righteous of one man (JESUS) makes all men who believe forgiven, because God brought Lot and his house out. So why did the lord bring judgement on Sodom and Gomorrah? The Spirit of Religion would have us think that it was because they were gay or homosexual. The bible doesn't say that. What does the bible say?

It was because there was none righteous there. What is righteousness? Righteousness is right standing with God. Righteous in our day is not the same as it was in the Old Testament. It is the right standing with GOD, but the act by which one had to do to receive it or be accounted as to having it.

What is Right Standing in The Old Testament

In the Old Testament doing animal sacrifices was and act of faith that covers ones sins for one year, which was to believe that Jesus or the seed of the woman would come and crush the head of the serpent. Where did this start?

It started in the Garden of Eden with Adam by God the father and passed down in the book of Genesis. It is seen clearly with Abel in the 4th chapter and fourth verse when it talks about the fat there of, and with Seth. The fat was burned on the altar and had a sweet smell of sweet savor, which is the lord Jesus. When Noah had gotten off the ark the first thing that he did was make an altar for the burnt offering. In the 8th chapter 21st verse we see that Noah did it and it was taught to the other three families that were to repopulate the earth. So all men knew it, but went away from it. We know that the Bible teaches that Noah's three sons repopulated the earth. Therefore the father was justified in bringing punishment to Sodom and Gomorrah as the judge of all the earth which Abraham said of the lord in verse 25 of chapter 18.

There was also MELCHIZEDEK, according to genesis 14:18 he was the priest of the highest God. The job of a priest is to intercede for men who were falling short of their responsibility to God that is in sacrifice. Man before Jesus came to the earth and died for man could not live sinless for he had a sinful nature and needed a bloodsacrifice. A Blood sacrifice is to cover their sins from judgment, judgment would not come on them as it did in Sodom and Gomorrah. Did the king of Sodom and the king of Gomorrah not know who Melchizedek was? How did Melchizedek know what had happened with Abraham to bring the wine and bread? He blessed Abram and Abram gave the tithe. Abram had been paying the tithe to him, as did others.

What is Right Standing in The New Testament?

Right standing for the New Testament believers is to take it to be the truth, by faith that Jesus was our substitute or our propitiation by faith. The bible says that God the father has laid on JESUS the sins of us all. Jesus bore our sins and sickness as Isaiah 53 says starting in verse 3-11 and

2nd Cor.5: 21.

God has made Jesus to be sin for us who knew no sin that we might be made the righteousness of God in him. (this is covenant)

When anyone comes to God and asks for forgiveness, confess that they are sinners and ask that Jesus come into their hearts, they then get the gift of righteousness. When a person does that (confess Jesus as Lord) they are clean by the blood of the lord Jesus. Their spirit is clean of SIN Nature and death. A new nature of Divineness which is Love, and Eternal Life is then given to them and they are clean in their conscience of guilt so the person can stand in GOD's presence and feel that they have never sinned before, which is righteousness.

In Romans1: 18 Paul talks about this very thing and in that verse. Paul speaks of the word unrighteousness. Where did Paul get this from? The Old Testament, and From the Holy Spirit, because there was no New Testament. You should read the whole chapter from verse 18-32 so you can see for yourself. There is the whole understanding of the men of today that profess Christ and uphold homosexuality that is in the church, but they are not apart of the body of Christ. This also is the way it was at Sodom and Gomorrah, that is why judgment came on them. Homosexuality is a choice, and that is their God given right.

We know that homosexuality is a choice because when a child is born, it is not gay, it is male or female. Nothing else

People who choose to be gay will not tell the truth and accept the responsibility of their actions. But will say that they are a female in a male's body or the other way around with a male in a female's body and that God has made a mistake, not them. Not accepting them is sick, homophobia. phobia is a sickness They make you and any that will not accept them as having a problem.

When God makes a mistake, we men are in trouble. What they are really saying is that they are God and know better than the creator does. For when man finds God's mistakes, he then is THE MOST HIGH GOD. And if you know where the mistake is you know how to correct the mistake. So they think the correction should be made in the body, so they get an operation, but the bible states that in spirit there is neither male nor female (gal 3:27) which makes them wrong. They don't know how to get the spirit changed where the mistake really lies. When the truth is they're believing the lie of a lying spirit because somewhere in their life they decided to do what they did for whatever reason and wants everyone else to accept that it is apart of life when it was not so from the beginning. The other reason the lord did what he did is in second Peter 2:6 which gives an example to those who would live ungodly.

Righteousness is a part of our son ship that gives us the right to fellowship with GOD. Righteousness causes our faith to work it makes the kingdom of darkness to obey us as part of the kingdom of heaven with Jesus as king of it, who scepter is a scepter of righteousness understanding what a scepter is. This is just a small part of righteousness which fight the spirit of religion of the things that it is doing to the kingdom of heven and the sons of GOD.

Another lie from the spirit of religion is the world was made in seven days as in twenty-four hours. When it was actually seven thousand years. The sun, moon, and stars were not made until the fourth day, read Genesis 1:14. In the beginning when the Jehovah said "let there be light." This is *speaking*, not creating the sun. Verse 3. And the sun is not created until the fourth day, which sets the twenty four-hour periods that we know today. So what is this that is being done?

2nd Peter 3:8, one day with the lord which is one thousands years which no man has lived. So the world as we know it was made in seven thousand years, not a twenty-four hour period. When Jehovah said to Adam "the day you eat of the tree of knowledge of good and evil (not an apple tree) you shall surely die, In that twenty-four hour day Adam died (was separated from God the father) in that one thousand years Adam lived to be nine hundred and thirty years old.

Here again we as the children of God do not know what death is. We think that death means no more being, but death is being separated. We are spirits, we have a soul, and we live in a body.(eternal spirits) 1 Thess, 5:23, the very God of peace sanctify you holy and pray God your whole spirit, soul , and body be preserved blameless until the coming of our Lord Jesus Christ.

Spiritual death is separation from God; Physical death is the spirit separation from the body. The body is buried and the spirit goes to eternity, Heaven or Hell. The bible speaks of the second death which is permanent separation from God with punishment which we believers will not take part of. Born again believers do not die, we fall asleep. Look at Acts chapter 7, the story of Steven and in the end of the story it speaks of death but the bible says he fell asleep, verse 60.

If you will look in the Strongs Concordance under sleep, you will see all that sleep with their fathers. And still another lie of the spirit of religion that causes the body of chirst to be divide.

A big one, about Adam eating of the tree of good and evil. First Jehovah gave Adam a choice. Genesis 2:16, every tree you may freely eat of. *Every,* means all trees. He had the choice the entire time, because God the father gives man free will, to love him and obey him. The spirit of religion does not want us or man to see him (GOD), as he really is, our father how much he loves us. Then the father tells his son if he does eat of the tree what would happen as a parent does. The father gives Adam the choice to obey or not to obey. God was not trying, to be God, but a father. Have you not done this with your children or loved ones? If you have read this and understand, you should be able to feel the broken heart of the father, his love for you and his love for man.

The first thing that the Jehovah gave to man was life, then he gave him choice. Life is all about choices; it is what a person chooses life or death. (Where you spend your eternity) The father says chose life. There are those who do not know that there were men and women on the earth before Adam. There were Cities of which Eden was. The fallen angels carried on with these people, the cave man. If you can receive this, look at the sixth day when Jehovah created man God the Father is creating by speaking. The father made them male and female, and tells them to be fruitful and replenish the earth. This is to say people had been before them, you cannot re-anything until you have first done it before.

Moses tells us about the father making Adam after the day of rest. Adam is God's son who is ruler over all men, and to understand how woman came to be, God shows us that he took the bone of man and created woman. If Adam and Eve had all the babies that were on the earth at that time then Eve must have been a baby making machine. And that would mean Cain had to have married his own sister, which would make that incest, and God would have placed him in it, which we know God would never do. So who were the people that Cain was afraid of? Where did he get his wife from, if there were no other people on the earth? From whom was Cain talking about when he says everyone that finds him shall slay me. Then the lord says whoever slays Cain; vengeance shall be taken on them sevenfold. In verse 21 we find out about the harp and organ players or pipe players this is music I say a band, and according to the word Cain built this city. In chapter 6 we see the fallen angels got involved. This was the intrusion to the human race, which brought wicked giants in the earth that helps bring the flood on the earth.

Now the spirit of religion has used this and many other things to keep the body of our lord separated on things like being spirit filled, speaking in tongues, baptisms, and the Lord 's Supper, I could go on and on.

So where is this in the bible and how does one learn this? (the spirit of religion and this teaching) I came by this by the Holy Spirit. Listening to Gloria Copeland, she said the lord had told Oral Roberts to read the four Gospels and the book of Acts three times in thirty days, which I did, and in the third reading, that the Holy Spirit began to tell me of the spirit of religion

That it was many spirits operating over the denominations to keep people out of the promises of God. Which most denominations do, even though they say that they believe the whole bible, but don't. They argue over being baptized in the Holy Spirit and being filled with the Holy Spirit.

To ask anything about being baptized in fire, they know nothing. Most will tell you its being filled with the Holy Spirit. Most believers or those who are born again have not been baptized in fire, for only Jesus can do this. Matthew 3:11, say they are not the same. They will say that they are, because they have not experienced it and was told that is was being filled with the Holy Spirit. They never ask the Holy Spirit themselves, taking what someone else has told them. Now go ask the father and see what he says.

In the book of Matthew 3:7, Pharisees and Sadducees had come to the baptism of John the Baptist, why were they there? They were there to witness the word of God coming to pass and see the Christ. (Messiah)

THE PHARISEES

The Pharisees were a sect. They believed the angels, other spirits, and in the resurrection. They were moral, zealous, self-denying, and self-righteous.

THE SADDUCEES

The Sadducees were a sect that denied the existence of angels, other spirits, the resurrection, and miracles. They were the most sect in the Sanhedrin and the priesthood.

To believe there is no resurrection is to say that you can live any kind of way because resurrection speaks of judgement. Judgment speaks of there being a God to whom we must give and account to and for the things done in life. First how we treated others? Then to what we had, and what did we do with what we had? And how we got it? Then how does this affects us today? Most denominations teach that being born again is you get the Holy Spirit at that time but that's not the truth. When a person is born again his spirit is cleaned and he gets a Devine nature, and ask that the lord Jesus come in to your heart which cry out father to Jehovah. In the blood is life, and the blood is able to speak. Hebrews 12:24 tells us that Abel and Jesus' blood spoke. After a person is born again he needs to be baptized with the Holy Spirit. Being born again you become a child of God when a person becomes baptized in the Holy Spirit he gets the fullness of the spirit that helps him to becomes a Son.

A child speaks of immaturity,(Gal.4:1-7) but a son gets his inheritance; he gets about his fathers business. A son understands who he is, what he has, and what he can do. A son knows that at the cross he used 2nd cor, 5:21 confessing that he was a sinner and he needed God. He did not know to forgive himself for his sins, and take it to be true that what God the Father did in Jesus on the cross and when he finds no signs of old life that he has been forgiven, Col 1:12-14 so that he can go in the Holy of holies and sit at the right hand of the father and rest Eph 1:20-21.

Most denominations teach that you need to come to the preachers not your father, for John wrote you have no need of a teacher for you have the Holy Spirit to teach you. Son ship is gained through prayer and study of the word so that when you hear the word preached you can tell if it's the father and you won't be deceived.

This is to say that all denominations fall in one of those groups. How come they don't speak in tongues? Peter and Paul did, because of the teaching of the denomination, not the bible. I will not call the names of the denominations, which do these things because God is fixing that. Now there are men in those denominations that are speaking in tongues and laying on hands anointing with oil and confessing they were wrong (glory to god) which are not of the Pentecostal teaching of the Bible. This is the body of Christ coming together. I don't know what sister Gloria calls it, but I call it power reading. What I call power reading is to read the four gospels and the book of Acts three times in thirty days. To help you do this you should mark your bible in times, that is the first time, second time, and third time.

You mark it in eleven chapters a day. It takes two days to read a book. See that the lord will tell you things you've never heard before. I know it seems like we've gotten away from the faith subject, but we haven't. You have to know these things to understand why people think that Hebrews 11:1 is what faith is when it's not. Its how faith works.

You must remember that the word understand means to know how a thing operates. The understanding of a person having faith is being able to change any circumstance with just their words, or that I have the ability of GOD This level is intercession, also the second phase of Jesus' ministry which he is doing now. We will look at the power that it carries with it to understand that when you use it, what you are doing and what to expect. The intercessor is taken into the Godhead as lawyer for man, and asks that the judgement that is to come be changed and mercy be given so that what ever the person asks for will be done.

The intercessor is to understand binding and loosening, Mathew 18:19. Because most believers don't know this, so their love one stay in sin for years binding and loosening carries **authority** with it caused by a revelation The prophet is GOD's voice to man, the priest's is man's voice to God. In the Old Testament the high priest went to the holy of holies once a year with the blood of bulls and goats to cover the sins and stay the judgment, which it did until Jesus came. All believers can act as intercessors and there is an office of intercession which only the Holy Spirit can place a person in. that gives a person prayer assignments to pray for people or places or even things. First let's look at Abram who was and intercessor.

In Genesis chapter 12:13. Abram said to Sarai, "say that you are my sister to keep my life," which caused Pharaoh to take Sarai to make her his wife, and caused the lord to plague the house of Pharaoh. Here some would say that God does not do this kind of things but verse three of this chapter say he would. Look at verses 17-20, hear the fear that is in Pharaoh, that pharaoh spoke; he didn't want the things back. In that account Abram did no intercede.

In Chapter 20 we find this happening again, (the taking of Abraham's wife) the difference is Abraham has cut the covenant and understand what faith is. we found out why pharaoh was in fear. This time it was Abimelech king of Gerar, who has fallen into fear of GOD. We find out that the lord went to Abimelech in a dream and said you are a dead man cause of the woman, she is a man's wife and Abimelech pleads his case to the lord as a righteous man, and even as a righteous nation which he was king over. And Abraham interceded for him that we see judgment changed. Now there are three spiritual classes that are in the spirit realm, so we may understand our selves and why we have faith.

The Spiritual Classes

SPEAKING SPIRITS

The first, is speaking spirits, second, non speaking spirits and third, fallen spirits. A speaking spirits have the ability to create things, as Jehovah the father made them to be. The non speaking spirits, the servants of God not having the ability to create. The fallen spirits are just fallen angels that have become outlaws, and the kingdom of darkness. Man was created to be Gods son, he was made in the class with his father and whether he knows it or not, he is the cause of his own troubles with his own mouth, caused by the not knowing of the laws of faith and that he is in the class of speaking spirits.

THE LAWS OF FAITH

In the begaining of this book, one of the things I talked about was that romans 3:27 which talked about the laws of faith. A lot of us have heard these laws but were not told that they were laws. I have heard great ministers speak on them but not put them together as the laws of faith which we will go into as the laws of faith that speaking spirit need to understand.

Proverbs 18:21, death and life are in the power (AUTHORITY) of the tongue. This is the first law of faith.

Proverbs 21:23,

Who so ever keep his mouth and tongue keeps his soul from trouble.

we have to understand the revelation of James from the book of proverbs

JAMES, 3:5

James said it best in verse 5 chapter 3, from the book of James, the tongue is a little member and boasts great things. In verse 6 James says the tongue is a fire, a world of iniquity, so is the tongue, among the members that it defiles the whole body and sets it on fire of hell. This tells us that the tongue is what causes what happens in our life's and our world, and our self-talk (what we say to ourselves about ourselves mentally)

In the 12th chapter of Matthew, Jesus tells us that a person speaks when his heart is full. Full of what faith or fear, again Let's look at Job.

JOB 3:25-26

25. for the thing which I greatly feared has come upon me, and that which I was afraid of has come unto me.

26. I was not in safety, neither had I rest. neither was I quiet yet trouble came.

Job was full of fear, so he spoke that into his life and world but did not speak evil of God and his self. The whole book of Job and the trying of his faith was to see if he would curse God, which Satan was trying to do but failed (test job's faith). For Job's confession was though he slay me yet

I will trust in him, so we see that the test of faith is what you say about God because he is listening and says if you get promoted

Job 13:15, which was, Job's passing the test, because he had not cursed God, and as always the devil is a liar. Look at Jobs ending, Job had twice as much as he had in the beginning(the fight of faith is over the things that you have (family, money, and your health) and the lord had Job pray for the three friends who needed an intercessor. Job's promotion was from priest of his family, to priest for men. This tell us that at times Satan get to test our faith

Now lets look at Moses in the book of Exodus, we will see Moses as an intercessor acted as an advocate (person who pleads for another; attorney.) Moses tells the lord that what others will think about him if he should not show mercy, and in verse 14, the bible says the lord repented of the evil which he thought to do unto his people. As you can see that this was for a whole nation.

In the 23rd chapter of Luke we see Jesus our lord as he intercedes for those that are crucifying him and he intercedes for them to Jehovah as he says "forgive them for they know not what they do. Intercession is all about the ignorance of the sinner. In Leviticus 4:22, the rules are sinning through ignorance. This is what intercession is all about, the ignorance of the sinner, to give them mercy, but a person must have faith, to do so.

I MET A MAN

I met a man, if he was a man or an angel I do not know, but what I do know is that he had a strange affect on me, and the thing that happened with him, his name was Sidney Blackwell.

While I was in Vietnam I spent seven months in the field then I was assigned to the third of the thirteenth Headquarter Company, where I did special duties for headquarters and headquarters company. I brought women and men on base camp to clean and do other odd jobs.

One of my assignments was to build a truck wash. I had to dig a hole in the ground and put a water tank in it. It was to be ten feet long and eight feet wide and eight feet deep. Sidney was assigned to help me.

Sidney Blackwell was five feet six and had a smile as big as the Grand Canyon. Black, as we called him was assigned to me as a diver and as helper, with the people that we brought on base. Sidney had been sent to the Headquarters Company from the infantry, the second of the twenty-seventh wolfhounds.

When we were working at the truck wash site, Black always talked about the Jesus, and I did not want to hear that, He'd ask me to dig some but I would not. He just kept digging and talking. As I laid on top of the ground my back began to hurt, as Black dug my back hurt more and more. So I dug, and as I did the pain went away so I dug more, but I returned to my old self thinking that it was just all in my mind, But it came again as I just let him do all of the work with the men and women that we brought in at the time. I know that it was not in my mind, this was really happening, as I thought. So I took a turn and went back to work. This was the first time that supernatural things had happen, that I had notice

SHOT IN THE HEAD

Then came the dream that had brought me to Vietnam as I had thought. We were off work, we had eaten, and we sat outside of our hutches on the sandbags getting high (smoking weed), this is what I did every night. Black started to talk about Jesus he was telling me that he was having a hard time believing what he read in the bible, He asked me, "Do you believe that Jesus fed five thousand people with just two fish and five loaves of bread?" He asked "Do you believe that Jesus fed four thousand people with seven loaves and a few fish?

There were other people there; I asked if they were hearing what black was saying? I did not want to hear what Black was saying. Just a short ways away from us were howitzers firing and I had just come from the field and to hear them go off did not scare me. I didn't want to answer his questions, so I felt I would just go. Just as I got down off of the sandbags, one of the guns went off and I heard a voice inside of the boom. The voice said to me "SIT DOWN." So I did, and again Black asked me about the bible. He said he was having a hard time with believing that Jesus walked on water and raised the dead. The guys that were there said that they'd heard it before and didn't want to hear it.

But he wasn't talking to them, just to me. Again he asked "Mac, do you believe that the bible is true? And if so why?" I answered "I do, because its God word." He started again, asking me did I believe Jesus walked on water, raised Lazarus from the dead, and why did I believe Jesus fed 5,000 people with only two fish and five loaves of bread. Again I wanted to leave, because I was trying to get high and did not want to think about God and things like that.

I went to leave, and again the howitzers went off, again I heard a voice in the boom say

"SIT DOWN!" I sat down, and the third time Black asked me, did I believe the bible and the question of did I believe that Jesus walked on water? Yes! Did I believe that Jesus fed 5,000 with just two fish and five loaves of bread? Yes. and that he, raised Lazarus from the dead?

Yes. He asked me why. "Because it's God's word." And when I said that, in myself I heard a voice say I have found Jesus, whom I'd been looking for.

I jumped off of the sandbags and was going to grab and kiss him, and shout "I have found Jesus!" When a hand of fire came out of his chest and a voice from the fire said to me "stop He's not Jesus, whom You're looking for, he's just telling you of him." I stopped. I walked away saying to Myself "the voice that I heard with in me did not come from my head. I knew something Happened, it was the dream I was shot with the gospel. I was never the same again, from then on, neither did I know what faith was, nor the understanding of having it. Even though I had used faith as others had, not knowing what faith was and understanding having it.

To understanding faith. First we have to have the right definition, and the right understanding for having faith, the right understanding goes into the renewing of the mind, and understanding that faith has laws, which takes us back to the laws of faith, which comes from us being speaking spirits. We are spirits and spiritual law rules over all things for all things were made by the spirit Jehovah, the most high GOD. He set the laws , so we have to first know them, and second understand them as the bible tells us.

The just shell live by faith, that is a commandment. Here are the laws, and where they are in the bible, in the short story that I just told of my life that it was my faith that took me there, and the change of my faith confession that I refused to die, and the dream that God had given me came true, I just did not know that the bullet was the gospel.

The first law is life and death are in the power of the tongue, and we seen the revelation that James had gotten from it to teach to the new Christians that were baby Christian which we Already spoke on (child &son) which I had started on above as the lord had taught me, he showed me that I had used faith and not known it because I had not the understanding nor definition

THE FIRST LAW
Death And Life Are In The Power Of The Tongue.

The number one means source of GOD is always first or number one for he is the source of everything.

In the book of proverbs there are plenty of verses that speak of the mouth, lips, and the tongue.

All of them go with the first law of faith, such as proverb 21:23

Proverb 21:23 who so ever guards his mouth and tongue keeps his soul from troubles,

Proverb 6:2 you are snared by the words of your mouth you are taken by the words of your mouth.

All the scriptures that talk about the tongue, lip, and the mouth all fit in the first law.

In 1970 on Fort Gordon GA. Is the army base that I was station at when I return from Vietnam after being there some months I got in to a fight in which I was charged with assault with a deadly weapon and an temp to kill. I was sent to the stack Aid, and waited for a court-martial not knowing what was going to happen many of the prisoner who had received their court-martial had been sentence was telling me about the person that had gotten them convicted and that he had lost only one case in all of his military career, That I could look to go to prison for about ten to fifteen years, But I would not hear that kind of talk and said that the prosecutor would resign and become my attorney after being there about thirty days, I was put in salutary confinement for talking in the chow line for breakfast.

There I decided I would fast, and read my bible, and that is what I did. I did not want to eat dry pancake for breakfast or cornflakes with no milk. I would not drink water. I became dehydrated.

In the military court they give you a list of attorney that you should selected from. I refused so they could not take me to court that I know of. The prosecutor sent for me, I told him why I would not select my attorney, he ask why him? My answer was he was the best that I had heard of and that he was my choice. He asked who was the person that I was accused, of assaulting.

H J.(The person that had the fight with) and that was the only person that he had lost to.

At the time I talked to him, I did not know that till after he accepted me as his client.

When I was put back on the compound all the prisoner gave me the title as king of the compound because of what I had said, had come to pass. (when you use your faith you are king of your life, Job 22:28, you shall decree a thing and it shall be established unto you.) Because ETB (Earl T Barry) had

In the first draft of this book I did not understand that you could use your faith and not know that you were doing it, till God had shown me this for I was about to write that without the clear understand you could not use your faith which most of us have done, and sometime are doing now

Norman Vincent Peale understood this law he saw it as positive thinking for the law says Death and life are in the tongue which he saw it as negative or positive thinking which it is and brother Peale wrote many books and I had read the one "you can if you think you can" which I loved and still do because it is law one.

The Second Law Of Faith
Confession

Your confession brings you the possession Romans 10:9-10.

Romans 10:9-10. That if you shell confesses with your m outh the Lord Jesus and shalt

Believe in your heart that God has raised Jesus from the dead you shalt be saved.

10. for with the heart man believe unto righteousness and with the mouth confession is made unto salvation.

This is a very little known law by the church, and most have used it to be born in the church. I first come to know of it from brother Kenneth Hagen in one of his little book titled In Him.

Which teaches about who we are in Christ and throught our confession of faith we become that which we confess as Romans 10, 9-10 says.

In 1996, I and my three children live in Loma Linda California in our three bed apartment. I had no food to feed us. the children were in bed and for some reason I decided to mediate Philippians

4:19. **My God shall supply all my needs according to his riches in glory by Christ Jesus** as I mediated mentally from inside me the lord spoke and asked" am I your God"? hot Tears begin to flow from my close eyes I answered "yes Lord" HE said tell the refrigerator that. I open the empty refrigerator, and I realize that the empty refrigerator had been speaking to me spirit that we would die from hunger so I spoke that rhema word to the refrigerator that my God would supply all my needs that same day someone came and gave me $500 dollars. Law two confession brings you the possession of that which you are believing for.

Everyday we should do daily confession over our lives. There are three area that we should be confessing and they are our Finances', our Relationships , and our Health. These are the areas that the devil and his kingdom attacks, we seen this in the book of Job. Some faith churchs teach theses confessions. I AM WHAT THE BIBLE SAY THAT I AM. I HAVE WHAT THE BIBLE SAYS I HAVE, AND

I CAN DO WHAT THE BIBLE SAYS I CAN DO. This is the thinking Of the believers as sons of God. In the revelation of the lord's prayer, the second part of the prayer is hallowed be your name this is the place of praise the eight names of God that we are to confess over our lives. the eight compound names are 1. Jehovah tsidkenu meaning The Lord our righteousness having the right to come into his presence. 2. Jehovah M' kaddesh meaning the Lord my sanctifier. 3. Jehovah Shalom meaning the Lord my peace the word peace means that nothing is missing 4. Jehovah Rophe meaning the Lord my healer. 5. Jehovah Shammah meaning the Lord that is ever presence. 6. Jehovah Nissi meaning the Lord my banner saying that it is Jehovah who fight my battles and gives my the victory. 7. Jehovah Jireh meaning the Lord my provider. 8. Jehovah Rohi meaning the Lord my Shepard. These are the confession that should be made each day of our lives. Notice that they cover the three areas of our lives.

THE THIRD LAW
Meditation

THE third law a faith is to meditate. In Joshua 1:8 we are told to meditate the word of god. Meditation is part of the renewing of the mind which we are told to do in Romans12:2.

Joshua 1:8

This book of the law shall not depart out of your mouth; but thou shalt meditate therein day and night, that thou may observe to do according to all that is written therein :for then you shalt make your way prosperous and then you shall have good success.

What God say to one He says to all. So this is for us today as well, when we meditate

The word as Jehovah says the person who meditates shell prosper because meditation on the word of God is his delight. I told of how I meditate d the word and the out come was as God had said and then there is the forth law.

Law Four
Keep Your Heart With All Diligence.

Keep your heart with all diligence for out of it spring the issues of life. This verse tell us that when you are using your faith you must apply those laws, as this one say guard your heart, which is your spirit and remember that we are spirits living in a body and that we are told to guard it (our spirits) that is to be careful of what we let go in, because it will come in to our lives we should guard the gates to our spirits which is our eyes and our ears for words or pictures and they come in to our minds or the soul.

The soul has three part to it. the mind, the will, and the will the way it work is that words heard comes in to the mind that word are words cause pictures are seen on the screen of the imagination it is seen as we look we feel something about what we see and we then make a decision on it we like or dislike but when we are children some thought are given to us that affect us and think bad of ourselves and say bad things that causes bad things to happen this is law one death and life are in the power of the tongue, law two they confess it, and they think on it a lot which is a form of meditation, here is what I am saying, here an example.

Say a mother has a child and the mother had separated from the father and she now says things to the child like your stupid like your father and you will never be an thing the child only think that the parent knows what's right, and the child loves the parent so it believes what the parent says, and when the child makes a mistake it repeats the negative that the parent has said they reinforce the thought and say that they will never be anything so that is what the spirit dose for the life of the person that is why the fourth law of faith is guard your heart. But a child does not know this. nor how this work, that is why their life is the way it is. Now a person may hear this and think that they may change their lives with just by saying something positive one time are a little more but it does not work that way in the next part which is the language of faith. We will get a clear understanding of this.

LAW FIVE
The Lord Working With Us.

Law five states that the lord is working with us, Mark 16:20. They went out and preached Everywhere the Lord working with them and confirming the word through the accompanying signs. This law tells us that it is a partnership that is the partners both have a part to do we have a part to do and God has a part to do and we have a part, our part is first study the bible to know who we are in Chris tells us what we have in Chris and and what we have in Chris tells us what we can do and another part is that we must meditate and do our daily confession which renews our minds and because we do this diligently, our world changes and our life and the plan of God unfolds and we have the dream of our lives when we do the fifth law of faith we do the four that are in front of it. We read and remember the scripture this is our part and God the father will cause it to come to pass as to say he is with us by signs and wonders

LAW SIX
See Yourself With It.

Joshua 6:2

In the book of Joshua the eight verse the b part of the verse that says see I have given it to you. This is telling us to use our visualization. What is visualization? Visualization is the ability to see things in your imagination as I said before that when words come into the mind words are pictures and when we see them in or on the screen of the imagination we feel something about what you see, which causes a decision to be made.

Neville, a mystic and spiritual teacher, taught that visualization and faith were the two parts of Creation, and that it was in and a part of man, that we had this ability to use to make life better, the abundant Life. We are responsible for the use of it. Neville taught how to do this, and get that which you see yourself with and feel that you have it so the experience feel real to the mind and the more you go there the more you believe it. Neville wrote FEELING IS THE SECRET and through feeling we cause that which we desire to come in to our world. Neville tell many stories in his book RESURRECTION of how many did this, see and feel the things that they wanted.

Let us go back to the book of Joshua chapter 8 we saw in verse 1. That the lord said see that I have given into your hands the king of AI and his people and his city, and the land: verse 2. The lord tell Joshua what to see that! You shall do to AI and her king as you did to Jericho and her king. This Joshua did and brought about the victory as it was with Jericho. We must see ourselves with the thing that we are believing for.

LAW SEVEN
Praise, Praise The Lord, For His Mercy Endures Forever.

Seven is the perfect number which means mature spiritual maturity is to praise God for all things For God is good all the time and in every way. Even when we don't think so nor can we understand it.

Praise is a war tactic in the spirit, when we praise God it is because we are in a test are Have ask for something and believe that we have received it. We are to praise too keep our faith Growing because it says that we have it praise says thank you to our father. Satan have the right to test our faith. The test is always over what you believe you have and our praise says that we do even though others can't see it yet, that is why heb 11;says now faith is the substance of things hoped for, and the evidence of things not seen. Our Praise says to the father that we believe him that faith is the supernatural ability of GOD given to his sons in law six we see our selfs with it and in seven we praise because we take it to be true. The praise that they spoke was "GOD is good and his mercy endurance for ever"

In 2nd chronicles 20:-21 we are told that Judah is under siege by three of Judah's enemies, Moabites, Ammonites, and Edomites. Had come to make war against Judah and their king Jehoshaphat, but Jehoshaphat decided to seek the lord to know what to do? when you don't know what to do, what do you do? they were told not to worry are fear not nor be dismayed but to go out to battle their enemys. And the put a praise team in front of the warriors as they march to the battle and the enemy turned on each other because of the praise of Judah. The same thing can be seen when Moses and the children of Israel got in a battle with the Amalek when Moses raise his hands with the rod of God in his hands that Joshua and the Israel won the fighting for praise is a war tactic. This war tactic is against the senses 0f our body.

LAW EIGHT
Act As If It Is So. Joshua 8:2

Eight is the number of new beginning and the law is to see yourself with It, act as if it were so are you had it where others could see it even though they can't, you have it in the spirit ream that only you can go there and see it this law works with the sixth law. Because you see it and act as though it is cause the senses to stop the fighting your faith.

The fight of faith is done in the mine so the senses tell the mine that it is not real so that makes it hard to believe that it is but when you act as though it is the senses start to believe and your continual daily confession, and meditation, done daily helps to convert the senses to believe. This is what Paul was talking about in the seven chapter of Romans the war between the spirit and the body, for the body is ruled by the senses and this is where the devil deals with the person to get them to sin. This is also what Jesus said if you believe the things you say, you will have the things you say. When we confess that we are new creation in Christ we become that and see ourselves as that for somethings come faster than others.

LAW NINE
Look Not At That Which Is Seen, But That Which Is Not Seen. 2nd Cor 4:18

This law is also a visualization you must close the natural eyes to open your spiritual eyes and see what you want and feel it and practice the feeling as I had told you what I learn from reading Neville 's book feeling in the secret. when a person look at things that they create on the screen of the imagination, the senses are suspended. that is why we can have it in the subjective world bringing them to the objective world. Looking at that which is not seen helps to keep the senses or flesh from fighting the spirit for when you do this at times the senses say that it is just fantasy and fantasy is not real so you lose it as not being real,. But when you feel It, It tell your senses that it is real of which it cannot tell cause it felt it. So it does not fight the spirit, when you say that you have something, or that something is, and you live this way

LAW TEN
We Walk By Faith And Not By Sight

This is not living by your senses to get through life with out the things that the Father has given or said that he has done for us and to us by his word. This verse tell us to practice these laws

With every situation to walk by faith is to be lead by the spirit of God, the word of God says the son of God are lead by the spirit of GOD. This is talking about being mature and the word child speaks of immaturity,. In the book of Gelation the 4th chapter verse s 1-8 speaks of this of how a child becomes a son. A child is seen as a slave having no right to the promises of GOD, but the father sent Jesus in the fullness of time to change that, born of a woman born under the law to for fill the law and to redeem man.

THE LANGUAGE OF FAITH

The language of faith is I am, I have and I can do. The language of fear is I can't, I don't, have, I am not. When people speak they tell a mature son of God that they are a child and not a son.

In Norman Vincent Peale's books he always note that the persons he helped were not speaking faith but fear and that they were breaking law one and two they were speaking death and not life

They had a negative or bad confession law two bring the thing into your life because the person believed it. Jesus said if you believe the things you say, you should have what you say.(mark 11:23). We must know God and his ways his way is, what the father says to one he say to all.

To understand the language of faith, we must understand the different between what the bible calls a child and a son we spoke just a little about it but we need to look into it fully of what the bible say about a child, and about a son. the Father call the end of a thing long before the beginning before the worlds were form Jehovah had crucified Jesus which was the ending and what Jehovah had wanted done and his plan to redeem man, see the ending from the beginning Jehovah, Jehovah called Jesus a son not a child. "this is my son in whom I am well pleased" Jehovah called Jesus a son from the begaining speaking of him as being mature. Paul tells us of the child and how to spot them, paul said when I was a child, I spoke as a child, I understood as a child and I thought as a child. We can tell what you are by what you say, you speak faith or fear, and because of their understanding which is none at all they don't know what faith is, nor how it works.

Our understanding comes from our thoughts and that every thought is not your but some is from the devil that is why we are told to cast down imagination, and reasoning. This is part of the faith fight to not let thought take root in our mines for proverbs 20:11 says that a child is known by his deeds. Not only his deeds but what he says our word fram our worlds just as GOD the Father words framed this world so do our worlds that is why we are the God of our world.

Listen to what we are saying, and see if what we are saying is it not what is going on in our lives. and a lot of times people are saying things to us are trying to put things in your lives and they don't believe that it takes place.

In my work place a man got on the elevator and said we going down to hell ha ha ha. Some of the other people thought it to be funny but not me, I believe what the bible says is true and that you will have what you say. I said "no you may be going to hell but I am going to the basement of this building". Just a few months ago I tour my tendon the patellar tendom of my right knee that happen march 18 it was a big snow that morning, as I walk to catch the bus to work, I slipped and tour it, thanks be to GOD that some one came along and help me up and rode me to my house now my knee is healed and to day someone saw me and said jokingly "That I had a bum leg," I said" no I don't have a bum leg." People do not understand these things and how they work.

Everyone has angels, The good are call angels of light, and the bad or evil one work for the kingdom of darkness. Your ark angels give work assignment to the other angels their assignment work off of your words,

Law one of faith, Death and Life are in the power of your tongue. You are the God of your world for you are made in the image of the GOD. heb 11:3 say that we understand that the worlds were made by the words of Jehovah and we all have a world. Which is made by the words we speak, the good things that we say the angels of light go and find people that are in our world to give the things that we say.

When I lived in California I was trying to teach my mother in law faith. She heard me say that god would have someone give me a car, not that I just wanted someone to do that. it was what I needed to look for a job. Even thought she was born again and spirit filled, she did not understand and was full of unbelief, my mother inlaw, and my wife both keep saying it was not going to happen, as soon as she left our home, and my wife left the home, what I said come to pass.

A man from the church who was a greeter, meet me as I got off the church bus, he also not only give me the car to me, but paid to put it in my name, we talked, next Sunday he told me that the lord had told him to give me the classic Cadillac. He had bought, to give it to me.

This man I did not know him, nor what he knew about the lord, for in my time in prayer I said to the holy spirit "I don't know what he knows about you, but I receive the car father, you know that my license was suspended and I did not have the money to pay for them to be unsuspended" the next week at The church picnic we saw each other he pull me to the side, and said the lord had spoken to him to not only give me the car but to pay for my license to be unsuspended. only God could have told him that because I told no one what I told the Father I received the car and it help me get a job to help take care of my children and my self.

Later I ask the lord how come it did not happen when Barbara ann and her mother were in the home? He answer the two of them their words of unbelief could stop mines for they had two angels to fight one of mines but when they left their had to go with them so when we say thing that are full of unbelief it fight the good work of another that is believing.

There was a time that we were living in hotels and we had no money and barbar ann had use the car and we were put out of the hotel with all our clothes the holy spirit told me to put the clothes in a red basket and go and sit the down by a tree that was in between to gas stations my daughter America said she would go in the station and ask people for money to help pay for a room but I told her sweet heart we are children of GOD and we are not to beg for nothing.

I said God will Have people come and give to us that which we need there was a man who came and ask would we be fine, if he gave me the change he had , I said yes, the second person came and give me seven dollars and left he came a second time but he left he return a third time and called me to his car he said he had drove ten miles away and turn around twice he had a boat hooked to his car that he was to transport to someone about twenty minute away, but God keeped telling him to give me the hundred and fifty dollars in his wallet, but he keep saying to the lord that's all he had, he did not know how he was going to feed his family, but he gave me the money and went on his way, he said the lord told him" I was his brother and needed the money more than he did."

The man returned about forty five minute later, rejoicing he thought he would be late to meet the person that he was to deliver the boat to, but he was early , the man paid him a thousand dollars for the delivery and gave him a contract to deliver ten more that month at a thousand per delivery he could not believe want had happen, because he gave me his last, his all. He now had ten thousand for this month.

A third person came, this lady went and paid for the room went to the store cash a check and brought my back twenty five dollar. which made me have about two hundred dollars. My daughter said "dad we did not have to ask any one for money."

Jesus said" if you believe the things you say you will have whatever you say" that's law two your confession brings you the thing you believe. This is why you have to understand language of faith. It tells you if the person is a child of God or son and be careful of what other say about you and them and even what they tell you to do.

A lot of Christian like to say take care. They do not know what they are saying to you for they don't understand words for them to tell you to take care is to tell you to sin. For the bible says case your care over on the lord. If you took care, you would not do as the bible tells you cast your cares on the lord, but you disobey that is sin. Christian who say that think they are wishing you well as god of our worlds our words frame our worlds words are the most important things in the world for the world were made with word of Jehovah and were made in his image and his likeness. We do things his way.

Hold i

If you will read in the book of number we find out the children of Israel did forty years in the wilderness in their murmuring said would God that we had died in Egypt or would God we had died in this willness! This is what they said and this is what happen to them, but Caleb Joshua said something different they said we are well able to take the land when all over twenty and up died in the wilderness. But Caleb and Joshua went in to the promise land forty years later. When a child of God grows up they know to watch their month for it is what brings the cures or your blessing.

THE PURPOSE OF FAITH

Why did the Father give us faith? Knowing that it is his ability! It was so that we don't have to do as the religious church does in some churches they teach that you have to ask God to do this and do that for you and that is not what the bible really teach luke 10:19 Jesus said behold I give you power to tread on serpents and scorpions, and over all the power of the enemy; nothng shell by any means hurt you. In this verse the lord makes a statement that he had given us power over all the power of the enemy.

What power does Satan have, and where did he (satan) get that from? well Satan got his power from Adam, who was the first son of God on the earth, and he was the god of this world and when he eat from the tree of good and evil, the eye of their understanding was open, that's how they, he and eve know that they were naked. Adam was the God of this world. When we look at Adam in genesis we see this when he spoke to the animals and they came to life, God had formed their bodies and brought them to Adam. Adam had a word of knowledge, Adam know the thoughts of God as he formed the body of the animals. those were the second animals that were made none of the pre historic animal were put on the arc. Because the number two means to establish Adam was the second man which meant he would establish the family of god on the earth but he did not, Jesus did. he was called the second Adam. So that we understand where Satan got his power from which Jehovah had given to Adam who in turn gave it to Satan. So what was Satan's power?

Satan had the power of death, sickness, and poverty, which is the curse of the law. Because Satan was the God of this world he did as he wanted act 10: 38 the b part tells us that, it says (Satan) who went about oppressing the people. Jesus healed them who were oppressed of the devil.

Then the purpose for Jehovah gave us faith so that we would be as he is a God, because the word God means the user of supernatural ability when you have supernatural ability you don't have to ask the Father to do for you that which you can do for yourself that is why you never hear Jesus ask for things that he could do. The lord only ask the father to do that which was in the father power like put him (Jesus) back in the Holy GOD HEAD. Jesus asked in the 17th chapter of John and in the first chapter of Hebrew verse 8 it is done. read Hebrew 1:8 Jehovah calls Jesus a GOD (big G) give him a thrown , a kingdom, and a scepter of righteousness. Jehovah's purpose of giving us faith is to asure that we win every battle that we come up against 2nd Corinthians 2:14 GOD WHO ALWAYS CAUSES US TO TRIUMPH FROM VICTORY TO

VICTORY it's because of faith. Calling those things that be not as though they were.

Here is a question for you, If God gave you power to do what he could do why would he do that when he knows that you can do that for yourself. Why did you teach your children to tie their shoes so they could ask you to do it for them? NO so they can do for themselves so when you can do it you do it and you whip the devil just as Jesus did.

ALL THINGS WORK BY FAITH

You must use your faith to be victorious in the Christian life, as the word says the just must live by faith and if it's not faith it is sin. We have been given faith to live victorious in every part of our lives, in our health, in our relationships and in our finances. Because of our sonship we have authority which is by faith that we run the devil off when we fill our hearts or our spirits with this authority of who we are and where we seated this will drive out all sickness for all sickness is in the spirit for we are spirit beings 1st Thessalonians 5:23 whole spirit soul and body. The three parts of man. So when we are sick it is our spirits and the word tells us this in Proverbs

The four chapter starting at the 20 verse to 22nd and it reads

20. MY SON ATTEND TO ALL MY WORDS; INCLINE YOUR EARS TO ALL MY SAYIN YOUR HEART OR (SPIRIT)

22. FOR THEY ARE LIFE TO THOSE THAT FIND THEM , AND HEALTH TO ALL YOUR FLESH

healed from every disease and from every sickness, for the word is God. It will not give place to lies are sickness when the person does as he has said.

In our finances we have to tell the devil to take his hand off our money and claim. the amount we need and tell the angels to go and cause it to come in being patient it will as we claim. By faith we say that we have it.

In our relationships we have that power to drive out kingdom of darkness off of our lives and love ones, that they may be free. This is the understanding of what faith is, and the understanding how to use it for faith is for the house hold of God. Now how do we get faith? We know what Faith is the parts of faith , how faith works, it purpose of our havinging it now where can we get it from? There are two kinds of faith Rhema and logos

Rhema

The word Rhema means the spoken word of Jehovah to a person when Jehovah speaks to a person they get faith. The bible teach faith comes be hearing and hearing the word of god this is not the only to get faith you can get faith from the word of God, the bible to get faith from the bible is call logos and the different is that with rhema the faith is ther as he speaks but with logos you have to mediate on the word that you want to get the faith out of. First lets talk about rhema as I had said that paul states that faith comes by hearing and hearing the word of God,

When we want to really understand faith we have to study father Abraham who is called the father of faith, it is through him that we first understand faith and getting the definition of what faith is, and to understand that you have to believe God and not to listen to others reasoning as with Abraham when he Jehovah, had told him that he and his wife would have a child. Abraham heard right, he told it to Sarah. at that time Abraham told this to his wife, their names had not been changed to Abraham and Sarah to cause the child to come,

Sarah in her unbelief it could not happen they were old now so she (Sarah) thought that her Husband heard God wrong and that Abraham should take second wife to have a child with, but she was wrong, and this brought many problems to the whole world.

Then there came a time that Sarah heard God say that she, Sarah would have a child she laughed but she had faith and because she heard a Rhema word and got faith to have the child for God had asked" is there anything to hard for God?" that is how Paul knew that faith comes by hearing and hearing God.

Now logos has to have mediation mix with it, spent time with the word to get the faith out of it as a person spends time meditating on the word the spirit of the word will speak to the person meditating the world. Meditation gives to the meditator and application, the application brings about a manifestation when a person does the application, they gets a super natural happening or what is called a **Miracle. Yes the faith that Jehovah has given us is able to do that** we are more than able to handle whatever life would bring mark 11:22 have the faith of GOD.